Celebrating NHL time with nature festivals and skyblue partying and funny sports doing

Impressum:

Bibliografische Information der Deutschen
Nationalbibliothek: Die Deutsche
Nationalbibliothek verzeichnet diese Publikation in
der Deutschen Nationalbibliografie; detaillierte
bibliografische Daten sind im Internet über
www.dnb.de abrufbar.

© 2020 Peter Oberfrank
Herstellung und Verlag
BoD – Books on Demand , Norderstedt

ISBN 9783751924733

This book „Celebrating NHL time with nature festivals and skyblue partying and funny sports doing" is a happy being book with good memories and enjoying and with heart.

House red heart and church Rapperswil

House Mickey mouse and woody house

Disco palace house

Gardenhouse and sporting house

Space shuttle house and flower house

Sporty house

New York Rangers house

NHL american indian feder house in Montreal

Hamburg sea house in
marmorstonebetonwoodungo styling
so calling 2 floors villamarmoring

Sports stadium Montreal village

Australia flowering house

Opera housing so calling specht
houses and palm trees in the garden

Zürichsee theatre house and school
and kindergarten

Rosen House with celebrating music
partys ….. playing flipper and disco
dancing and philosophy evenings and
enjoying nature and sports doing

Rome cathedral house

Napoli white golden palace

Bergamo forrestmarmor house with beaching

Hunziker family house in Rapperswil

Sporty stadium in Hamburg and modern villas houses and dancing with the mouses …..

Zürich party house in colourful style and dancing with the cats and the hats

NHL stadium orange wood styling houses worldwide

Germany stylish harmony
woodstyling marmor house

Rapperswil church bell ring house
with beach being and dreaming …..

Calgary flames house with sporty being

New York stylish unique house with wood and iron and marmorstone and steppyramiding nearby harbour and NHL homey Madison Square Garden

Rapperswil Märchenhaus

Washington stylish unique türkis library house

St. Louis browning style house and wide range beach and steg and flowerland and treeland and christmas land and easter land and icehockeysportshall

Miami smiling marmorig house with forrestveranda and flowergardening and seabeach and waterbachelen and palms

Las Vegas dessert house in dschungelland

Amzonas housing with meeting all pets and all plants with treassenbalcoons and wide natureland

Arizona mountaineous housevilla with one stock living and grande veranda

New York central park stonehouse
with great balcoons and big
natureland and sporty land

Nashville villagiongo house in woody style and great ofen and sey view balcooning

Rapperswil sports palace

Montreal icegarden housevilla

Toronto beach hotelhousing

Ottawa almhüttelehousing in mountain walking area and seas houses and burghouse

Los Angeles Kings beachhousing

San Francisco gardening sea betoniron housevillage

Boston bienenhousele with cherrish balcooning and tentsbuildings

Detroit discostadele

Chicago american indian woodstone
housing in high comfortable
tenthouses on big meadowsealand

Vancouver modern fashion housing

New Jersey woodforrest housing and teicheland and small mountains area and waterfalls

Philadelphia in butterflyterassen with
10 stockwerken beautiful housing
and schilfsealand and moosland and
grassland and stonesland

Luen city Indianerhaus colourful styling

Buffalo stonewoodyhouse in easy styling and meadowlooking enjoying

Minnesota adlerhorst housing constuructionwoodbeton with 5 stockwerke and comfortterassen and happy celebrating with the coffe and tea tassen and cocosnuss and tv show „Wetten dass ....“ and hills land and seaside looking

San Jose opera house living with marmorrosastonish betoning and wood land

Colorado mountaineous house and Vail holidaying

Carolina creative housing with
marmor and colours

Florid beach ressort housing with
palm wood celebrating and housing

yeahi brown wood and
skybluestonegrey housing with 2
stockwerken and glamorous
balcoonverandas and uniquee colour
meadow and church veranda on the
ground floor

NHL housing christmasing and eastering and celebrating with betonmarmorarchtitectual triangle styling

NHL museum village with woodymetal construction in artfull forming

Tampa Bay ligthning opera house
and sporty stadium with sea and
beach being

NHL puck house in Africa

Moskau happy and smiling palace

Klagenfurter Athletic Club colwnig
housing in colourful gymnastic
styling and good partying and natural
feeling and enjoying garden areas

Dallas rosa villa with wood and
lounge balcoons for dreaming and
being and moon and stars looking
and beachside sportsstadium

Edmonton flowerlava woodhousing with betonstylish and small ofening and joyful sportyarena

Winnipeg surrounded by hills lucky dancing palace living with stepybalcoons and pyramidish styling and gardening

New York Island big veranda stylish woodymarmorig living with smily being

Anaheim luckylen duckilen living in big grounded villas with palmwood and medium ofeles and triangle sportsstadium and beachressort and dschungelland

Pittsburgh hills beverly villa marmor

NHL soft marmor style house

Rapperswil sporty opera theatre cinema dreaming enjoying palace with dancing